Original title:
The Porchlight's Glow

Copyright © 2025 Creative Arts Management OÜ
All rights reserved.

Author: Nash Everly
ISBN HARDBACK: 978-1-80587-088-3
ISBN PAPERBACK: 978-1-80587-558-1

## Lantern of Dreams

In a yard where shadows creep,
A cat took a brave leap.
It aimed for a mouse, oh so spry,
Landed in a pie, oh my!

The moon chuckled up above,
'What a mess, where's the love?'
With whipped cream on its tail,
The cat now tells a tale.

**Safe Harbor in Darkness**

Under a sky full of stars,
A raccoon pilfered candy bars.
He thought he was clever and sly,
But ended up stuck in a pie.

The porch light flickered, gleamed,
As the raccoon loudly screamed.
With sugar stuck on his nose,
He danced, in a sugary pose.

## Night's Gentle Embrace

Fireflies waved, a spark of cheer,
As kids in pajamas drew near.
They caught one in a jar, oh so bright,
Turned it into a mini-nightlight.

The jar rolled away with a clink,
It's off to explore, I think!
The kids burst out in a laugh,
As it guided them down the path.

## Call of the Hearth

S'mores toasted by the blaze,
A little dog begs and sways.
He thinks it's a fair trade,
For a bite of marshmallow made.

The fire crackled, leaving no doubt,
The dog tripped and fell out.
Covered in chocolate and goo,
He barked, 'Can I try some too?'

## **Illuminated Reverie**

In the night, a bulb burns bright,
It flickers, it winks, a silly sight.
A moth does dance, oh what a fool,
Chasing light like a kid in school.

Laughter spills from neighbors near,
As shadows play with goofy cheer.
A cat does pounce, but misses the mark,
Creating chaos in the dark.

## Shadows of Forgotten Dreams

Under the lamp, a silhouette strays,
Spinning tales of olden days.
With each chuckle, the shadows groan,
Making noises like a brass trombone.

A sock puppet's on the scene,
Making jokes that are quite obscene.
Who knew that fabric could be so wise,
In this ridiculous masquerade of lies?

## **Warmth Beyond the Glass**

Outside the window, the world is cold,
But our jokes are worth their weight in gold.
We sip on cocoa, giggles ensue,
Critiquing each marshmallow like it's brand new.

The dog's asleep, a soft little snooze,
Dreaming of bones and silly ruse.
While we create more nonsense and cheer,
That's when the neighbors come crashing near!

**The glow of a thousand stories**

Gather 'round, it's story time,
With wild tales and a dash of slime.
A chicken walks into a bar, they say,
And the punchline wobbles in a funny way.

We're all convulsing in fits of glee,
While the cat rolls over, but not for free.
For every laugh, a scratch on the back,
In this whimsical world, there's no lack!

## Solitary Flames in the Night

A candle danced on the sill,
Swaying gently with free will.
It flicked and flared, oh what a sight,
As it tried to win the battle of night.

The cat leapt up, gave a curious stare,
Knocked down a vase, didn't care, oh where?
The flame wobbled, then laughed with glee,
For now it was a circus, you see!

## Lanterns of Remembrance

Grandpa's lantern always swayed,
Filled with stories that never frayed.
He'd sit outside, spinning tales quite bold,
About the time he wrestled a bear—so the legend told!

But last I heard, it was just a dog,
And the flare he fought was just a fog.
Yet we believe in the stories grand,
For laughter is what connects this band!

## Flickers and Fables

The lights on the porch flickered near,
As I attempted to catch a ghost here.
But instead, a raccoon took a seat,
And a game of charades was soon to greet.

Under the glimmer, he acted quite sly,
For the snacks I'd set out made him fly!
Alas, the fables of ghosts went away,
Replaced by the rascal munching on hay.

## The Lure of Evening's Light

A streetlamp glowed with a disco flair,
As neighbors swayed without a care.
The light buzzed tunes that made us prance,
Until the dog joined in on the dance!

With a woof and a wag, he stole the show,
Tripping the posts in his flashy glow.
We laughed till we cried, what a sight to behold,
Evenings like these are pure comedic gold!

## **Essence of Nightfall**

As shadows stretch and giggles rise,
The moon sneezes, much to our surprise.
Crickets chatter in a wacky tune,
The stars wink at us like a cartoon.

Neighbors argue over which cat's which,
While dogs are busy plotting a switch.
Fireflies dance like they've lost their keys,
Creating chaos between the trees.

## **Whispering Lights**

Glow worms gossip, sharing their tales,
While a raccoon steals snacks, leaving trails.
Laughter echoes under the moon's gaze,
As we reenact those childhood days.

Our shadows twirl in silly ballet,
Chasing away the dark, come what may.
With every chuckle, we add to the scene,
As wild as a dream on a bed of green.

## Heartbeats of the Evening

In the soft hum of the cooling night,
Socks and sandals give quite a fright.
Yet here we gather, all mismatched styles,
Making memories that'll last for miles.

The grill smokes up the plot like a chef,
Muffled giggles serving a humor clef.
We toast to the stars with mugs of cheer,
Cackles and snorts, a regular smear.

## Glow of Togetherness

Here we are, a misfit crew,
Seeking warmth in each other's view.
Stories fly like popcorn at a show,
And laughter's the wind beneath a bow.

As twilight softens and crickets play,
We'll dance to the tune of nightfall's sway.
With every chuckle, the world feels right,
In this jumbled glow, we find our light.

## Glows at the Edge of Night

In the dim light, shadows play,
Cats on patrol, in grand ballet.
One tries to catch a butterfly,
While others just watch, oh my, oh my!

The raccoons stop for a late-night feast,
Raiding bins, they're quite the beast.
They tip over cans with nimble grace,
Thinking they've won a wild goose chase.

The dog barks loud, a valiant knight,
Defending turf till the morning light.
While squirrels snicker from their high perch,
Plotting pranks with no need to search.

Under the stars, the laughter spills,
Echoing softly over the hills.
In the night's glow, fun freely flows,
At the edge of night, whimsy grows.

## Soft Shimmers of Belonging

Socks missing, where did they go?
Maybe the dryer's now a show!
Each sock with a story, bright and bold,
A tale of mischief, or so I'm told.

Neighbors wave with awkward cheer,
In pajamas, they appear so dear.
A late-night chat about lost shoes,
And the neighborhood gossip that never lets loose.

A cat parade struts down the drive,
With attitude, they thrive and jive.
Each one claims a spot, tails held high,
In this wild world, they're all the why.

Over laughter, the moon takes flight,
Winking down, it joins our night.
With silly stories and heartfelt cheer,
In shimmers, we find we truly belong here.

## Conversations in Half-Light

Under the glow, secrets unfold,
Between the whispers, laughter bold.
A frog jumps in, thinking it wise,
While the crickets play mood music, no disguise.

Old chairs creak with tales of yore,
As friends recount moments they adore.
Like when Fred tripped on his own shoes,
Causing giggles, like popping balloons.

The distant hoot of an owl calls out,
As if joining the fun, without a doubt.
And in the shadows, ideas brew,
Here in the dim, friendships renew.

Every story hides a little jest,
In this half-light, we're at our best.
With silly thoughts and charming wit,
In laughter's glow, we all brightly fit.

## **Resilient Rays in the Dark**

When night falls, shines a little spark,
A pesky fly buzzing, oh how it barks!
Dancing circles around a friend,
Every flap adds to the night's blend.

Dreams mingle with shadows, quite absurd,
The owls hoot stories, not a real word.
Sipping tea like lords and dames,
Discussing the weather in silly games.

A midnight stroll where the lunatics roam,
Finding adventures, almost like home.
Laughter echoes, a delightful sound,
In this cozy corner, joy is found.

The fireflies twinkle, a radiant team,
Lighting the way, creating a dream.
With each chortle and spark, we embark,
On a journey of fun, where there's no dark.

## **Beacon of Solace**

In the dusk, a bulb winks bright,
A moth's loud dance sparks sheer delight.
We gather 'round with snacks in hand,
Telling tales that are far from grand.

As shadows stretch and giggles grow,
A sudden breeze makes curtains flow.
The dog barks loud, a cat meows,
While neighbors frown and raise their brows.

With every joke, the bulb may sway,
As laughter spills into the fray.
We spill our sodas, trip on chairs,
Each clumsy move, a joy we share.

So here we sit, beneath the glow,
In laughter's light, our spirits grow.
This space a realm where all is clear,
With snacks in hand and friends so near.

## Warmth in the Night

The light beams down, a compass bright,
 As bugs join in, a dance of flight.
We swap our tales, both bold and lame,
 Proclaiming victory in silly games.

A shadow flicks across the wall,
 Then cats appear to join the brawl.
We laugh so hard, we almost cry,
As lightning bugs put on a show, oh my!

Each laugh echoes through the night,
 While fireflies glint in merry flight.
With mugs of cocoa, we feel so bold,
 Finding warmth in stories told.

So raise a cup, let's toast this tale,
Where humor rules, and naught can fail.
In the glow that warms our hearts tonight,
 We'll dance together in pure delight.

## Flickering Whispers

Softly murmurs in the dark,
As shadows play, we hit our mark.
A flicker, a giggle, a sudden pause,
One tale leads to a round of applause.

A neighbor's cat jumps in our midst,
Causing chaos with a hasty twist.
We share our secrets, one or two,
While moths flap by shouting, 'Boo!'

A candle tips, revealing grace,
As we all burst into space.
A chorus of laughs, a clink of cans,
In the night, confusion plans.

So here we sit, beneath the stars,
With funny stories and silly jars.
We are the crew beneath this light,
Flickering whispers take flight tonight.

## Beyond the Threshold

At the door, a warmth does call,
Across the yard, we begin to sprawl.
With silly hats and tunes that soar,
We tell tall tales and always want more.

The clock strikes one, we're still awake,
Wondering how much noise we can make.
A sudden crash and all eyes turn,
As popcorn flies and chairs all yearn.

Uncle Jim breaks out his old guitar,
Strumming melodies, we cheer from afar.
He sings about a cow and a shoe,
All the while, we're lost in the view.

So here's to nights so full of cheer,
With laughter louder than we can hear.
Beyond the threshold, our spirits blend,
In a glowing night that knows no end.

## **A Safe Haven in the Darkness**

When shadows creep and whispers sigh,
The light, it seems, knows how to fly.
With snacks in hand, we brave the night,
Laughter echoes, a comical fright.

The critters dance, with wild delight,
As I trip over my own two feet.
A battle of wits with the moths ensues,
I swear they're plotting, sharing their views.

The stars above play hide and seek,
While I recount my awkward streak.
It's a café for bugs, or so it seems,
As they feast on my late-night dreams.

Yet here I stand, embracing the show,
With popcorn in hand, let the antics flow!
In this cozy nook, I'm the shining star,
In a tale that's goofy, near and far.

## The Dance of Faint Flames

In flickering light, we find our moves,
With shadows swaying, the body grooves.
A jump, a twist, I step on a shoe,
The laughter erupts; it's nothing new.

The flames crackle, as if they know,
The rhythm of chaos we invite to grow.
With friends beside, we twirl and glide,
No such thing as grace; it's the wild ride!

I show a spin, and someone falls,
In the dance of disaster, everyone calls.
We paint the night with our silly prance,
While the moonlight watches, joining the dance.

In the glow, our troubles are few,
Just goofy moves and laughter too!
Under the stars, we spin with glee,
Until we collapse, just happy to be.

## Traces of Light and Love

The glow beams bright, yet it flickers still,
As I tell a joke, and all hearts fill.
With every chuckle, the night becomes real,
In this light, we share more than a meal.

Forgotten fries, oh where did they go?
I trip over them, putting on a show.
Friends point and laugh while I search the floor,
It's bound to happen, just once more!

The light plays tricks, on the walls it dances,
As we make plans, concocting odd chances.
In the warmth, we spill our tales so odd,
It's more than just light; it's a bond with a nod.

With snickers and giggles, our hearts do align,
Creating a glow that's perfectly fine.
In this space of joy, we fully embrace,
The traces of light, love, and our place.

## Horizon's Embrace

As night unfolds, we gather near,
With stories to share and a bit of cheer.
The horizon yawns, and so do I,
As I almost drop my drink—oh my!

We bask in moments; they never grow cold,
With pranks and giggles worth their weight in gold.
The moon's a witness to our comic spree,
As I lose a shoe, that dear old me!

The stars twinkle, snickering at our plight,
While I try to dance, but stumble with fright.
Yet here we are, in this cherished space,
Where laughter lingers with a warm embrace.

In the glow of laughter, dreams take flight,
We toast to the silliness under moonlight.
A gathering here that's full of fun,
As our silly antics rise like the sun.

## **Illuminated Haven**

A bulb flickers, buzzing loud,
The neighbors wonder, and laugh, so proud.
Cats chase shadows, in the light's embrace,
We trip on shoes, a comical race.

Friends gather round, with snacks in hand,
In this bright zone, all is grand.
Jokes fly high, like moths to flame,
Laughter echoes, it's all a game.

The dog barks loudly, trying to play,
A squirrel steals chips, what a display!
We cheer the chaos, with drinks in tow,
In our lively scene, there's always a show.

As dusk arrives, we're still in cheer,
Sharing mishaps, year after year.
With each funny tale, our spirits grow,
In this radiant space, we steal the show.

## **Shadows of Comfort**

The light above, a beacon bright,
Illuminates the late-night fight.
Who stole my fries? It's a grand debate,
Squealing laughter, oh, it's fate!

Ghosts of jokes from times before,
Resurrected here, who could ask for more?
A dance-off starts, with moves so bizarre,
In this bright circle, we're all a star.

The cat leaps high, a ninja unseen,
Crashes the party, it's quite the scene!
We yell and cheer, in mirthful spree,
With shadows around, we feel so free.

In this crazy place, where wonders flow,
We find our joy in the light's warm glow.
With each silly moment, we end the night,
In our cozy haven, filled with delight.

## Radiance in the Dusk

As the sun dips low, the glow shines bright,
Making even squirrels look funny in flight.
We sip our drinks, and the stories unfold,
Of wild adventures, and mischief bold.

The lawn chair wobbles, a daredevil seat,
My buddy flips back, what a goofy feat!
We laugh till we cry at the folly of fate,
In this luminous space, nothing feels late.

The glow bugs flicker, like party lights,
While neighborhood dogs engage in their bites.
A race around, we join in the chase,
All paths lead to fun, in this quirky place.

With every chuckle and burst of glee,
We find that in laughter, we're truly free.
As the light fades softly, we still hold tight,
In the playful dusk, everything feels right.

## Embrace of the Twilight

Twilight beckons with a playful cheer,
Bugs swarm about, and I sip my beer.
Footloose and fancy, we kick off our shoes,
In our bright patch, we all share the news.

"Who can balance?" a challenge declared,
We wobble, we giggle, who really prepared?
The chaos ignites as we tumble and roll,
In this cheerful haven, we're on a stroll.

A firefly lands right on the pie,
Is it dessert now, or just a sly spy?
Sibling rivalry joins in the fun,
What starts as a prank turns into a run.

When darkness falls, we don't say goodbye,
With shadows around, our spirits fly high.
In this twilight realm, where friendships bloom,
We bask in the laughter and light from the room.

## Timeless Flickers of Remembrance

Sitting here in socked feet,
My neighbor's cat dances to the beat.
I swear it's plotting a heist,
For the fish that swims, so not so nice.

Flashing back to summer nights,
When bugs flew in, oh what a fright!
We'd howl like wolves and make a mess,
Chasing shadows in our Sunday best.

With lemonade, we'd take our stand,
A potent brew from the kiddie band.
Our giggles echoed under the stars,
While our dog critiqued from our old cars.

Now the memories flicker and tease,
In the gentle whisper of a cool breeze.
But no, I still can't find my shoe!
And the cat? It's still plotting, it's true.

## Glow in the Calm of Twilight

As dusk unfolds, the laughter spills,
A cricket choir gives me the chills.
The fireflies dance, all aglow,
While I trip over my garden hoe!

A drink in hand, I toast the night,
To friends who mix up wrong and right.
With tales of glory, they boast and brag,
But all I see is their soggy rag.

Around the glow, a troupe we make,
As funny fumbles cause a quake.
With chips in hand, we start the roast,
On who ate all the dips, not a boast!

With laughter curling like smoke in air,
We share our secrets and silly flair.
As the stars wink and giggle, too,
I'll never outlive this cream stew.

## **The Light that Binds Us**

In the yard, the lantern sways,
Lighting up our goofy ways.
A sing-along with no right tune,
As we scare off the raccoons by noon.

Chase a rogue glow through laughter's veil,
With every joke, I tell a tale.
Though my punchlines often fall flat,
If you can't laugh, well, you're just a brat!

We gather here with snacks galore,
As wild stories earn us a score.
A taco fight erupts in glee,
Now we're all one big, messy family!

From birthday gags to shadow plays,
We cherish those brave, silly days.
Here's to the light that binds us near,
And the jokes we share year after year.

## Afterglow of the Heart

Evening falls and silliness blooms,
With feather boas and silly costumes.
A dance-off starts, I twist and sway,
Then trip on the rug and shout, "Hooray!"

Laughter lingers like the night air,
As I reminisce with an overdramatic flair.
"My cat's a lawyer!" I blurt out loud,
While my friends cheer me, goofy and proud.

The snacks we share, there's far too many,
A pie fight waits, oh, isn't that plenty?
We reminisce about the times we fell,
As secrets spill, oh do tell, do tell!

In this joy-filled afterglow we sit,
With hearts so full and quite a bit of wit.
In our little world of crazed delight,
We find our peace in this silly night.

## The Allure of Glistening Paths

When the moon takes a stroll in the sky,
Socks with sandals appear nearby.
Everyone's searching for the lost cat,
It's just napping on a comfy mat.

Laughter echoes beneath the big tree,
A raccoon sneers at the sight we see.
With ice cream cones melting too fast,
Sticky fingers remind us of the past.

Bikes are parked in a wobbly line,
Some kid thinks he's a real porcupine.
Pedal-powered chases, what a delight,
Under the stars, we'll race through the night.

We giggle at tales spun anew,
About the neighbor who once flew.
In this chaos, joy finds its way,
In glistening paths, we happily play.

## **Lanterns of Connection**

With flickering flames in hand, we roam,
Chasing shadows away from home.
A wayward beetle joins the spree,
While we dance as if setting free.

Giggles bounce off the garden brick,
Toads perform tricks that make us tick.
Our flashlights flicker, costumes collide,
Is that a pirate or a hole in the tide?

We link our arms, a train of cheer,
What's a small bump when fun is near?
In tangled tales, we weave and shout,
Connecting hearts, that's what it's about.

When lanterns dim, we'll not despair,
For in the dark, friends will always share.
With laughter echoing deep in the night,
These bonds glow bright, oh what a sight!

## Soothing Murmurs of the Night

Crickets compose a funny tune,
While the dog thinks he's a raccoon.
Under the stars, the soundtrack's set,
A sneeze erupts; wait, was that a wet pet?

Whispers float like balloons in the air,
With marshmallows burned, we shan't repair.
The moon's our judge, laughing with glee,
At all our goof-ups, yet we're still free.

A wise old owl hoots from a branch,
As we break into a curious dance.
In our yard, the wild things play,
Laughter lingers—hurry, don't delay!

We cuddle in blankets, the night wears thin,
With tales of squirrels who dream of tin.
Soothing murmurs, mixed with delight,
In these moments, everything feels right.

## Glows of Tomorrow Forgotten

The fireflies twinkle with mischievous cheer,
Turning the night into disco, oh dear!
Whirling around in a mad little spree,
Who knew nightgowns could double as capes, whee!

Tick tock, the clock laughs at our plight,
With socks still on, we cling to the night.
In pillow fights, old inner children remain,
Wrapping us up in a blanket of grain.

While cats roll their eyes at our silly games,
Our captured glows carry outout their aims.
Tomorrow might come with responsibilities, true,
But tonight we're just kids, and let's make it two!

So let the world spin its serious plans,
We'll conquer the stars, with our silly hands.
In this moment, let worries be light,
As the glows of tomorrow slip out of sight.

## Flickering Hope in the Night

A bulb that winks, then has a fit,
A dance of shadows, it won't commit.
Insects swarm like they're at a ball,
Yet I just sit, watching it all.

Neighbors peek with curious eyes,
Wondering if it's true, my plight lies.
No real party, just me and my snack,
With every flicker, I might go whack!

The light buzzes 'doom,' I hear it say,
Just flick it twice—no worries today!
What's that? A moth? A tiny orb?
Is it there for love or just to absorb?

So I laugh and wait for the next light's show,
'Cause anything goes in this brightened glow.

## Luminance of Longing

This old porch, where dreams take flight,
A lamp that blinks—what a silly sight!
Where wishes dance atop each beam,
I hope someone notices my gleam.

I wave to cars that roam on by,
Looking for a family—or at least a pie.
A cat saunters past with utter disdain,
While I recount my hopes, much to my pain.

The glow is bright, yet I'm alone,
Do I really need this buzzing tone?
Perhaps a friend or some cool flair,
To keep each thought from despair's snare.

Yet here I sit, stuck in my rut,
With jokes and smiles that seem to strut!

## Echoes of Twilight

Twilight whispers, the moon's on fire,
Yet my light just flicks, a failed desire.
I call for help; my neighbors laugh,
Can't fix the bulb, or plan a craft?

Oh, dear friend, come share this glow,
A game of charades? Or a poetry show?
But alas, it flickers—hold that thought,
A light that teases, while I've just fought.

The echoes sing of mischief past,
Under the glow, laughter's cast.
Could it shine brighter? I simply wish,
But hence comes a roach—my evening dish!

So I wave a napkin, a valiant knight,
We waltz in shadows, a comical sight!

**Serenity on the Stoop**

On my stoop, I sit with pride,
The flickering lamp—a playful guide.
A gentle warm, though it does tease,
With every buzz, my mind's at ease.

Where'd my snacks go? A lost remote?
Under the glow, I roam and gloat.
Is it freedom? Or fruits of my fate?
Only this light knows, I can't relate.

The stars must wonder why I'm stuck,
Staring at shadows, full of luck.
Still, this porch serves up quite the thrill,
With my trusty flashlight, I'll need to chill!

So if you stop by, bring pie on a plate,
We'll feast under this light—no need to wait!

## Flickering Dreams on the Step

A moth flew by, doing the dance,
In a swirling mess, it took a chance.
Thought it saw a snack, oh what a jest,
But it just found the bulb, now it's stressed.

A raccoon sneaks in, thinking it's sly,
Swiping my chips as I let out a sigh.
With crumbs on its paws, it makes a retreat,
Under the glow, it's a comical feat.

The shadows stretch long, you can hear them joke,
As my neighbor's cat eyes my broken yolk.
With a flick of its tail, it aims for my shoe,
Oh, come on, I swear it just laughed too!

So here on the step, with laughter and light,
The critters around me put up a fine fight.
In this flickering glow, life's antics unfold,
With dreams on the step, brighter than gold.

## Luminous Hearts Collide

Under the glow, two hearts take flight,
But one trips and stumbles, what a silly sight!
With laughter erupting, they take a breath,
Each giggle a step, dancing with depth.

The fireflies tease, lighting up the scene,
While the dog next door plays the role of a queen.
Strutting on up, with a grand royal bark,
Even the stars seem to giggle and spark.

A couple of squirrels start a nutty debate,
About who holds the best acorn fate.
As the laughter flows like a sweet serenade,
In the shimmering light, nothing's delayed.

When luminous hearts collide in this play,
Every stumble and fumble just makes the day.
With bright eyes and jokes, they light up the night,
In a whirlwind of joy, everything feels right.

## Ghostly Whispers in Soft Light

In the dark of night, I hear a loud squeak,
Was that a ghost? Or maybe a freak?
Turns out it's my chair, talking back with a creak,
Oh, how it loves to join in when I speak!

With shadows that dance, the cat's eyes gleam,
In the moon's soft glow, it's quite a dream.
A kitten conspirator, it stalks down the hall,
Pouncing at phantoms, it gives me a call.

The breeze rustles leaves, whispering 'hello',
I chuckle and wonder who's putting on a show.
Every rustle and giggle, it seems to delight,
In this spell of the night, so magical and bright.

So raise up your toast to the ghosts on the prowl,
For every soft whisper brings laughter and howl.
In the ghostly embrace of laughter's sweet kiss,
Life dances along in a hilarious bliss.

## Fading Echoes of Day

As sunset fades, mischief takes flight,
Chasing shadows and giggles held tight.
I spot my old shoes, they're trying to run,
But the laces are tangled—oh, what fun!

The neighbor's dog thinks it's on a quest,
Barking at nothing, he's truly the best.
With every loud woof, he plays his own tune,
Under this twilight, he howls at the moon.

A child's laughter echoes, sweet like a song,
As they trip over fireflies all night long.
With winks in the air and silliness paid,
Every fading echo, a treasure is made.

So as day turns to night, join in the cheer,
For life's full of giggles if you just draw near.
In the wane of the light, our joys will relay,
With fading echoes of the bright closing day.

## Reflections on the Porch Rail

Sitting on the rail, half asleep,
My thoughts begin to twist and creep.
A squirrel teams up with a tired cat,
They plot to steal my snack, imagine that!

The mailman trips on a ghostly shoe,
While the old dog laughs, oh, what a view!
Spilled lemonade becomes a grand parade,
As fireflies join the merry charade.

Breezy whispers carry tales from afar,
Of dancing frogs and a wishing star.
Each chuckle echoes into the night,
As laughter mixes with the silver light.

## Twilight Tales Unspoken

Underneath the stars, there's quite a scene,
A raccoon dances in a tutu, so keen.
A cat complains, 'That's not how you groove!'
While the porch swing creaks, trying to move.

A moth flirts fiercely with my ear,
'Free drinks,' it claims, 'just over here!'
Jokes from the shadows begin to unfold,
As crickets chirp in a rhythm bold.

The breeze whispers secrets of summer's cheer,
Unruly stories that no one can hear.
A midnight feast, with ants in the mix,
Turns our picnic into a comedy fix.

## Light in the Heart of Night

At night the world feels awfully bright,
With shadows doing a jig, oh what a sight!
A raccoon's on skates, gliding with flair,
While I chase a moth without any care.

Puddles reflect the moon's silly grin,
As I stumble sideways in my old tin.
The owls hoot back, they're part of the show,
And the stars wink down, 'Keep your moves slow!'

My shoe's untied, it leads on a quest,
To the edge of the yard, it really is best.
I trip and slide, with grace of a stone,
But laughter floats gently, I'm never alone.

## A Solace by the Steps

Nestled by the steps, I find my peace,
Where the forgetful cat won't cease.
Paws on the floor, she sneezes aloud,
As a curious gnat forms its own crowd.

A tumbleweed rolls, with vibes of the wild,
The neighbor's dog watches, rather unbeguiled.
He joins my laughter, with a woof and a tail,
Making the quiet feel like a grand tale.

A light flickers softly, like a wink from a friend,
Echoing moments that seem to transcend.
In the stillness of night, silliness blooms,
While our little porch hosts the greatest of rooms.

## Stories from Afar

In the evening's warm embrace,
A squirrel steals a shoe lace,
Laughing as he makes his run,
Chasing shadows, just for fun.

A cat strolls by, a queen on high,
With a confident strut and a quirky sigh,
She snags a meal from a careless hand,
Declaring victory, just as she planned.

The mailman trips, there's a slip and slide,
With packages flying, he can't hide,
A bouncing bubble, a cheerful sound,
Mail scattered, joy all around.

Neighbors chuckle, the night unfolds,
Whispering secrets, stories retold,
In the glow, the laughter grows,
Every moment, a spark that glows.

## Warming the Coldest Night

Jack Frost nips, with a cheeky grin,
While I lose my scarf, oh what a sin!
Holidays near, the lights are bright,
With tales of mishaps that make me light.

A dog barks loud, only to yawn,
As I trip o'er toys left out 'til dawn,
His laughter echoes through the chilly air,
While snowflakes settle without a care.

Carolers come, they sing off-key,
Mixing up rhythms, oh can it be?
With each missed note, the laughter flows,
As we battle chills with warmth that glows.

And when the cocoa spills with glee,
Splashing laughter, oh woe is me,
Yet still we grin, embracing plight,
For nothing's warmer than this starry night.

## Ethereal Glimmers of the Heart

In twilight's hum, a dance begins,
A firefly's prance, oh where it spins?
Its glow a giggle, a playful blink,
As I ponder how strange we think.

An owl hoots loud, with wisdom's prize,
But I swear I saw him roll his eyes,
He knows too well, the game's afoot,
As squirrels plot from their leafy nook.

A shadow speaks, or maybe sings,
Of whimsical thoughts and silly flings,
Nighttime whispers, just a short breeze,
Tickling our toes with playful tease.

Under stars, our laughter swells,
With echoes of joy, like ringing bells,
Every glance is a sparkly start,
Crafting tales that warm the heart.

## A Warm Embrace of Illumination

In the corner, a lamp stands proud,
Bathing the room, a golden crowd,
Its light reveals quirks, a paw print here,
As chuckles cascade, filling our cheer.

A toddler spins, with socks askew,
His giggle ignites a spark anew,
Dramatic bows with a wooden sword,
Every little jest, a joyful reward.

Grandma's tales of yesteryear,
Of shoes that danced and brought much cheer,
Her wink, her grin, a playful tease,
Every story's a breeze that frees.

And while the shadows mimic our game,
The warmth glows bright, no two the same,
In laughter's dance, the world feels right,
An embrace of joy in the deep of night.

## The Welcome of Soft Illumination

At night, the bugs all gather 'round,
A rave in the air, no music found.
The lightbulb hums a drunken song,
While my cat dances; oh, how wrong!

The neighbors peek through curtains drawn,
Witnessing my light-infused brawn.
I juggle snacks with grace, I swear,
But drop them all—a true despair!

The shadows shimmy, a curious sight,
Creatures of night, they join the fight.
I laugh and shout, then spill some tea,
The porchlight winks, it's just me!

So if you wander, don't be shy,
Join my circus, don't know why.
Embrace the glow, it's all in fun,
The night is wild, our work's not done!

## **Serenity in Radiant Isolation**

In solitude, the glow is bright,
I'm the owner of all this light.
Sipping lemonade, I craft new views,
Talking to roast marshmallows, no blues.

The stars above just blink in glee,
While my chair wobbles quite precariously.
A squirrel drops by, gives me a stare,
Wondering if crumbs I'll share.

In this bright bubble, I reign supreme,
Imagining dinners from my wild dreams.
But tripping over shadows is my fate,
And here I sit, laughing at late.

Still, the gentleness of night remains,
With hiccups in thoughts and silly refrains.
A dance with shadows, a soft little jig,
With laughter, I twirl just like a pig!

## Vestiges of a Dimming Day

As colors fade and night descends,
A hot dog vendor comes, he blends.
I chase the twilight, like a kid on the run,
But fall on my face—oh, isn't this fun?

The fireflies twinkle like set jewels bright,
Chasing them round feels just right.
They seem to giggle, but I clash and sway,
Fumbling through shadows, what a display!

With each misstep, laughter ensues,
A one-man show in my neon shoes.
Dramatic flails and comic reprise,
Glimmers of humor in the night skies.

The barbecue smoke wraps me tight,
Like a cozy hug, in this silly fight.
So here's to blunders and midnight food,
In the death of day, there's always good!

## **A Glimpse Beyond the Veil**

Through this glow, the night is wild,
Peeking at lost dreams, like a child.
With every flicker, a secret chance,
To twirl under stars and mischief-dance.

Beyond the light, the ghosts conspire,
To launch a prank, igniting fire.
I'm an unwitting jester of the dark,
Embarking on warranties—oh, what a lark!

The moon whispers secrets, damp and keen,
While I juggle shadows, feeling serene.
A duck walks by, quacking in tune,
In the glowing chaos, I greet the moon.

So laugh with me at the sight unseen,
Where shadows dance in a midnight sheen.
Frolic with spirits, hold them dear,
In this amusing veil, I shed a tear!

## **Serenity in the Ember**

A flicker tells tales of the night,
With shadows dancing, oh what a sight!
Sipping tea while the moths collide,
A comedy show, nowhere to hide.

Neighbors complain of the chatter and cheer,
As crickets join in, they sound so clear.
A raccoon peeks in, eyeing my pie,
The best late-night snack, oh my, oh my!

So much laughter in the soft light sways,
With jokes that get worse, but still earn their praise.
I forgot my keys, now it's not so funny,
Oh wait, what's this? A text from my honey!

Every glow beams hope in no rush,
Where silliness reigns, there's never a hush.
As the stars play guard, I tiptoe in glee,
Wishing tomorrow will let us just be!

## Flicker and Flare

In the glow of the light, the fun starts to play,
With kittens that pounce, and dogs in the fray.
Who knew such madness could fit in one place?
A dance-off between jars, oh what a sweet race!

The fireflies wink in an awkward display,
While I search for snacks in a whimsical way.
A banana split falls, oh what a mess!
But laughter erupts; it's part of the best!

We roast marshmallows, but they catch on fire,
And giggles grow louder as I start to tire.
The dog takes a nap on the picnic spread,
While all of my friends now dance on their heads!

With night slowly fading and the moon's gentle stare,
We recount each story, each giggle and dare.
As dreams start to loom, what a jolly affair,
A night to remember, in the flicker and flare!

## Lighthouses of the Soul

A lantern swings low, the shadows now tease,
While whispers of secrets ride on the breeze.
With pillows like clouds, laughter fills the gloom,
As we play charades in the living room!

A lamp in the corner winks with delight,
To the tunes of old songs we dance through the night.
With every poor note, a grin finds its way,
As cats join the chorus, what a strange play!

The bigger the fail, the louder we laugh,
And who knew my cat could show off his craft?
With whiskers a-twitch, he starts on his spree,
A talent show pièce de résistance! Just for me!

Under this roof, where our quirks intertwine,
We bask in the glow of mishaps so fine.
With friendship at helm, we navigate the night,
In lighthouses charming, we dance 'til the light!

## **Afterglow of Memories**

Now the embers are warm, but the stories run wild,
Of mishaps and mishmashes that fate has compiled.
With flashbacks that tingle, and punchlines retold,
We bask in the glow, in moments of gold.

The cat's in the hat, though it's fishy and blue,
And Uncle Jim's tales turn stranger, it's true.
We snicker and snort, with popcorn in hand,
As we chew on the past, it's all quite unplanned!

A slip on the bench, the humor's in place,
With cake on my nose, a sweet sticky face.
But laughter keeps flowing, like wine in our cups,
It's a jolly good time, let's raise up our puffs!

And as the night fades, I smile at old friends,
With bonds made of laughter that never need ends.
In the afterglow hours, we weave a soft lore,
Of joy in the moments we cherish once more!

## **Golden Hues at Sundown**

Golden rays spill from above,
As we laugh like a carefree dove.
Chasing shadows that tease and play,
Who knew dusk could steal hearts away?

Neighbors peek from around the fence,
Wishing they had our fun, immense.
We dance like goofballs, twirl and spin,
Who would have thought? Let the games begin!

The barbecue's smoking, burgers in flight,
Our flip-flops clash, oh what a sight!
A cat joins in, judging our fun,
With a flick of its tail, it decides we've won.

As night creeps in, we hear a sound,
A raccoon rummaging around the ground.
With chuckles and snickers, we gaze in awe,
Who knew the critters could be such a draw?

## Echoes Beneath the Stars

Beneath a sky, scattered with dreams,
We swap tall tales of wondrous schemes.
Fireflies blink like a secret code,
As we ponder which route our lives strode.

The dog joins in, barking with glee,
As we reminisce while sipping iced tea.
Mom's old stories, a riot to share,
Who would've guessed she had 'the flair'?

A tumbleweed rolls, we start to race,
Rolling on laughter, we pick up the pace.
A game of tag, who could resist?
Even the moon chuckles, clenching its fist.

There's a crash and a clatter, oh dear,
A chair tips over, laughter fills the sphere.
Under the stars, our worries unfurl,
Just a bunch of fools in a silly whirl.

## A Glistening Hearth of Memories

In the backyard, stories take flight,
Where laughter crackles like sparks in the night.
The s'mores are melting, sticky and sweet,
As we fumble with chocolate, oh what a treat!

A game of charades, who's hiding behind?
With gestures and giggles, our antics unwind.
The dog shakes its head, with a look to say,
"Humans are strange, why act this way?"

A candle flickers, casting shadows that leap,
While we recount all secrets we keep.
Each folly and blunder, a gift from the past,
Oh, how we've changed, but the fun's built to last!

As the embers cool, stories still fly,
We tie our hearts to the night's bright sky.
With a final toast to each heart in this glow,
We gather our memories, all set to go!

## **Sentries of Light and Shadow**

Flashing lights twirl across the grass,
As kids run rampant, daring to pass.
Unplugged from the world, we bask and cheer,
Who knew such joy could be found right here?

With every glow, a story resides,
Of epic battles and laughter that rides.
A frisbee soars, but a squirrel has plans,
Daring our throws with cheeky demands.

The moon pops out, a curious friend,
Watching our antics that never seem to end.
With chips in hand, we toast silly grins,
Each moment cemented as laughter begins.

Even the stars join our fun little play,
Winking in sequence, "Don't let this sway!"
With shadows dancing and giggles so bright,
We are the sentries of joy in the night.

## Guideposts in the Gloom

In the dark, I trip and fall,
Stubbing toes against the wall.
Yet a beam shines bright and clear,
Laughter spills, buoying my fear.

Cats parade like they're the kings,
Chasing shadows, plotting things.
I wave a fist at sneaky mice,
Only to step in spilled rice.

Neighbors grin while I fumble,
Tripping on my shoelace tumble.
With a chuckle, they set sail,
Into their homes, I follow trail.

In the night, absurd and free,
Guideposts glow and tease with glee.
I dance beneath the starry skies,
Cracking jokes and wild highs.

## Welcoming Light

Open door with creaking sound,
A glowing bulb that spins around.
Bugs line up like a parade,
Wings a-flutter, ready to invade.

Smells of snacks waft in the air,
As I gather to share and care.
Friends arrive, a motley crew,
With stories fresh and laughter too.

I trip over a clumsy pet,
Spilled soda, a funny wet.
But the light shines through the mess,
Turning chaos into bliss.

Together, we toast the night,
To mishaps that brought delight.
In the warmth, we find our might,
Under welcoming beams so bright.

## Shimmering Reflections

The moonlight dances off the wall,
Casting shadows, shadows tall.
Jokes bounce 'round like rubber balls,
As we trip at each other's calls.

Reflections gleam with silly grins,
Each misstep a jest that spins.
We toast to moments, good and great,
As laughter bubbles in our state.

I tried to show off my new dance,
Only to stumble, what a chance!
Friends erupt in roaring cheer,
For every slip brings joy near.

Glassy giggles fill the air,
With shimmering moments that we share.
In laughter's light, we find our way,
Turning gloom to bright bouquet.

## Watchful Illumination

Under watchful beams we dance,
Stumbling once, perhaps by chance.
Who knew a glow could be so sly?
Mischief twinkling in our eye.

Socks that slide on polished floor,
Sent us flying, oh what a score!
In the light, our shadows loom,
Dancing wildly, making room.

Unexpected guests drop by,
Bringing chaos, oh my oh my!
With each quip, the night takes flight,
In the warmth of shared delight.

Stealing snacks, we laugh until,
The watchful light holds us still.
In the dark, with giggles close,
We find joy in every toast.

## Candlelight Conversations

In the flicker, shadows dance,
A chat with ghosts, oh what chance!
They giggle, tease, make fun of me,
Should I laugh or run, oh gee!

A candle spills its waxy tears,
As voices rise, they drown my fears.
I spill my secrets to the smoke,
And share my jokes with old folklore.

The wick is short, the laughter loud,
Each punchline draws a silly crowd.
A toast to woes and lighter thoughts,
With drips of joy, we laugh a lot.

So here we sit, in soft delight,
With shadows playing, oh what a sight.
A candle's warmth, a friend so tight,
In quirky jests, we chase the night.

## Colors of the Dusk

The sky's a palette, quirky hues,
It splashes pinks and silly blues.
I wonder if the sun is shy,
Or just too busy to say goodbye.

A squirrel in shades of orange glows,
Knows not it's art, just how it flows.
It wiggles, twitches, strikes a pose,
While I stand laughing at its show.

The moon arrives, all bright and round,
With sparkly jokes that know no bounds.
She winks and grins, then starts to spin,
And soon enough, our fun begins.

In this dusk, the colors play,
A canvas made by night and day.
With laughter swirling all around,
In every shade, the joy is found.

## Whispers in the Evening Light

Whispers float like leaves in breeze,
Tickling my ears, with playful tease.
They say the cat's been up to tricks,
And stolen all the neighbor's licks!

The glow around, it hums and sways,
With giggles shared, in silly ways.
A band of fireflies, dressed just so,
Play catch, then trip in their own glow.

The clock strikes nine, with winks and fun,
And makes me wonder what I've done.
A dance with shadows, off we go,
With laughs that spark like fire below.

In evening light, the secrets weave,
Of tales so funny, I can't believe.
Twilight giggles dance and twirl,
As moonlight grins, and brightens the swirl.

## Lanterns of Solitude

Lanterns flicker, casting light,
In solitude, they shine so bright.
I chat with bugs who buzz and sway,
Their critiques, funny, lead me astray.

A moth joins in, it flaps and flirts,
While I spill tea, it spills my squirts.
We laugh about the old lamp's fate—
It's life cycle, oh isn't it great?

The shadows stretch, with jokes to share,
While I recount my funny flair.
In this peaceful, glowing scene,
Where solitude becomes a dream.

With lanterns lit, the night aligns,
For laughter found in silly signs.
Together with my buzzing crew,
In quiet joy, the humor's true.

## The Kiss of a Distant Star

In the dark, a comet zooms,
While squirrels plot their little dooms.
A shoe flies by, it makes a mark,
Someone's mad—was that a lark?

A telescope that's slightly bent,
Shows neighbor Ed, in strange event.
He dances with a broom, quite wild,
Their cat disapproves, it's rather riled.

A universe of clumsy grace,
Jellybeans float in outer space.
Just like that sock on the roof,
We giggle underneath aloof.

So if you see a wobbly star,
Blame it on a weird guitar.
For in the night, we laugh so bright,
And fake our woes with pure delight.

## Keeper of the Night's Secrets

Beneath the moon, a figure creeps,
With chicken wings and midnight peeps.
He guards the tales of mice and cheese,
While wearing wands to grant a tease.

A shadow jumps, it takes a run,
Spooning with the laughter spun.
Come join the dance; it's quite absurd,
In this circus where dreams are stirred.

The crickets chirp a wild refrain,
As gnomes perform a prancing gain.
But when you hear a rubber band,
Just know that squirrels have a plan.

Secrets shared with a wink and nudge,
Avoiding wisdom's heavy grudge.
Together we unwrap delight,
In the mischief of the night.

## Fables Beneath the Foyer Light

In a world where amulets glow,
Cats conspire and curtains flow.
A tale begins of socks that fight,
Underneath the foyer light.

With every thud, a giant's tease,
While mice debate the fate of cheese.
A wobbling chair, it tips and tilts,
The sleepy ghost spills all its silt.

Whispers of pancakes filling the air,
Laughter bursting everywhere.
Fables told with silly flair,
A rose with legs, a lady fair.

The stories twist like licorice bends,
In the company of silly friends.
So gather close for the night's delight,
And dance beneath that glowing light.

## **Resurgence in Dusk's Veil**

The sun takes its final dive,
As we bring our joy to thrive.
A trampoline made of old bike tires,
Leads to laughter that never tires.

In shadows thrown by buzzing lamps,
A troupe of ants sets up its camps.
They march in sync, a wobbly beat,
Making feasts of crumbs—oh, what a treat!

With whispers of dreams on a breeze,
A festival of giggles teases.
So ignite the madness of the night,
As fireflies join our wild flight.

Under dusk's veil, we play and cheer,
Imperfect tales we hold so dear.
For in this time, with smiles we'll face,
The beauty of our joyful space.

## Reflections of an Evening Star

A bulb flickers once and twice,
It swears it's sharp as any vice.
A dance of shadows on the floor,
I swear it's chased a cat before!

The moths throw parties, they're so bold,
In the glimmering light, a sight to behold.
They gather round, a caper so fine,
In their little disco, they sip on sunshine!

Each twinkle teases, every glow does laugh,
As bugs join in a comedy gaffe.
They duke it out, it's quite the sight,
In the night's embrace, all's pure delight!

But in the end, what's the real score?
Was it just a bulb, or an evening encore?
With laughter echoing through the air,
We all join in, without a care!

## Carried by Gentle Illumination

From afar, it calls like a siren's song,
With a glow that surely can't be wrong.
The neighborhood creeps, what's that about?
A light that teases; we cannot doubt!

We gather outside, a curious crew,
To ponder the glow and what it might do.
It flickers like gossip, oh so sly,
As if it's waving, oh my, oh my!

A raccoon struts in without a plan,
Dramatically circling just like a fan.
With a swipe and a swat, it claims its throne,
Amongst all the lights, it feels right at home!

The neighborhood "light" fights the night so well,
As all of our secrets come out to tell.
And in this madness, we laugh and cheer,
For what's a few bugs when friends are near?

## Leaping Shadows in the Night

A shadow leaps as the breeze comes in,
Is it a ghost, or just my twin?
With fingers snapping, and laughter loud,
These "haunted" hues draw the curious crowd!

In the yard, the antics never cease,
A porous dance that looks like peace.
The spiders mock, their webs on display,
As critters parade in eccentric ballet!

What's this creature, oh such a sight?
It's just a cat, on a moonlit night!
It swishes and twirls, thinking it's grand,
With the glow of the light as its spotlight's band!

But oh, the crackle of the misplaced laugh,
Brings out more joy than a simple photograph.
Amidst the shadows, we tumble and play,
In the night's sweet embrace, we let worries stray!

## Messengers of Warmth

In the evening mist, they become our friends,
These glowing wonders that never offend.
With a luminous wink, they spark a cheer,
Creating moments we hold dear!

The glow-bugs flutter, they zip and fly,
With motion so lively, they grace the sky.
Their jovial laughter, a messy spree,
As they flit about, both wild and free!

Even the porch cat rolls its eyes,
At the antics that bring such surprise.
With a sauntering tail, it takes a glance,
At this radiant circus, a dim-lit dance!

So here's to the glow that lights our way,
And to all the antics, night turns to play.
Messengers bright, we raise a toast,
To the warmth of laughter, and friendships most!

## Radiance from the Threshold

A bulb flickers, buzzing bright,
Calls to critters of the night.
Moths in my face, oh what a show,
Chasing shadows, to and fro.

The cat pounces, then takes flight,
A chorus of yelps in the moonlight.
Neighbors peek, with curious eyes,
Wondering what's causing all the sighs.

My coffee spills, a slippery floor,
As I stumble out, can't take much more.
The glow brings joy, in the oddest way,
Like a circus act at the end of the day.

## Beneath a Beacon's Embrace

Under the glow that leads the way,
A raccoon-like bandit starts to sway.
He steals my snacks and makes a dash,
While I laugh and blame him for the crash.

The light hums softly, a serenade,
As I dance awkwardly in the glade.
The fireflies quip and give a cheer,
At a talent show that's quite unclear.

My shoes untied, my shirt askew,
All for a laugh, a silly view.
Beneath this light's amusing plea,
Who knew such joy could come from me?

## Shadows Dance at Dusk

As darkness dawns, the shadows prance,
An unexpected, silly dance.
A fumble here, a tumble there,
While my shoes have started to wear.

A squirrel chimes in, with a flip and a twist,
I can't help but laugh, it's hard to resist.
My drink in hand, I popcorn spray,
As the critters join in their wild ballet.

Under this light, I become the star,
Swaying awkwardly, not going far.
In a world that's dark, my antics flow,
Thanks to laughter that helps us glow.

## **Hearthside Reflections**

At hearthside glow, my thoughts collide,
With visions of snacks that can't abide.
A ghostly glow of marshmallow foam,
Turns my chair into a plushy throne.

I toss a log, and it goes astray,
An epic duel with wood in play.
The clang of metal, the pop of a spark,
As shadows leap around with a lark.

But laughter rings through the cozy night,
With tales of mishaps and silly fright.
Hearts are warm, in the craziest mess,
Hearthside reflections, pure happiness.

## The Radiant Doorway

A light that flickers, oh what a show,
Attracts all the bugs, can't find a way to go.
A moth takes a leap, thinks he's a pro,
And finds himself caught in the warm halo.

Cats take their stance, with eyes all aglow,
On the porch they sit, stealing the show.
They spot a lone fly, and their tails start to flow,
As they plot their attack in an absurd tableau.

Neighbors walk past, with a laugh and a blow,
They glance at the scene, peek in to bestow.
"Is that a dance party, or just for the show?"
It's just porch light antics, now don't be a 'no!'

But when morning arrives, and night takes a bow,
The world's a bit brighter, if only somehow.
With memories of laughter, we look and we know,
That life's just a series of comical flows.

## Nightfall's Embrace

As shadows creep in and the world gets still,
A prankster emerges, it's a real test of will.
The neighbors throw glances, their patience a thrill,
While a raccoon sneaks close, gathering ill.

"What's that up there?" a voice will declare,
"Is it bright sparkly magic or just a light flare?"
With giggles and jests, they all gather to stare,
At the evening's events, with much pomp and flair.

The moon winks with glee, it's a casual affair,
As a dog barks loudly, it's hard not to care.
The porch is alive with laughter to share,
In nightfall's embrace, not a truth or a dare.

Just echoes of joy, with a slight humorous glare,
Reminding us all, that friendliness is rare.
We dance with the shadows, unwound from our snare,
A whimsical life, full of smiles and flair.

## A Soft Glow of Welcome

A flicker of light spills onto the grass,
Drawing in friends, both the first and the last.
There's a squirrel on the edge, with his lookout class,
Holding court over snacks, not letting them pass.

"Is that pizza I smell?" calls a voice from the rear,
Followed by laughter, it's best with a beer.
In this cozy enclave, where there's plenty to cheer,
Every friendly gesture brings a smile without fear.

As stories are traded, and tall tales appear,
About the soft glow that draws all who near.
With a wink and a laugh, everyone's in gear,
It's a porch party now, nothing left to revere.

But as the night wanes, and the crowd starts to clear,
The sparkle remains, and we hold it so dear.
With fondness we recall, as home feels sincere,
That light on the porch chases away all the drear.

## **Glimmers of the Past**

Where the light shines bright, memories abound,
Of neighbors in laughter and quirks all around.
Each shadow a character, stories profound,
With every soft flicker, nostalgia is found.

"Remember that night?" the chorus will sing,
When a piñata burst forth, oh what a fling!
Filled with old candy, it became a king,
As laughter exploded, the memories cling.

A cat in a hat, what an odd little thing,
Thought it was fancy, like royalty's bling.
Chasing the light, how that feline would spring,
"Who needs a reason? Let's just have a fling!"

As the evening gives way, to the glimmers we bring,
It's moments like these that make our hearts sing.
For amidst all the giggles, and tea cups that cling,
We find joy in light, in this playful ring.

## Cradle of Quietude

In the stillness of night, I hear a snore,
My cat's dreaming loudly, what's he dreaming for?
Perhaps he's a lion, on the hunt for a treat,
Or chasing after mice, with two left feet.

The neighbors' dog joins in with a bark,
An opera of chaos, it hits like a spark.
My plants seem to giggle, their leaves in a sway,
As if they're saying, 'What a wacky display!'

Whiskers twitch as shadows dance on the wall,
While I ponder if I'll have breakfast at all.
The fridge hums a tune, a melodic swish,
As I scheme for a sandwich that's truly delish.

Amidst all the ruckus, I snug in my chair,
Imagining worlds that float in the air.
So here in this cradle, where laughter is free,
Life's simply a sitcom, starring little ol' me.

## Safe Passage

A moth flutters by, it's seeking a light,
Bumbling and tumbling, a comical sight.
It dances on windows, a clumsy ballet,
With dreams of a glow, it butters my day.

The door creaks open, it first takes a peek,
Then in comes a raccoon, with its mask so sleek.
It steals my last cookie, in swift little paws,
I can't help but laugh, it's breaking the laws!

My slippers go sliding, I trip in a flash,
Witnesses giggle, with snickers and sass.
In this chaotic waltz, I waddle and sway,
Life's a grand circus, come join in the fray!

Safe passage through laughter, with stories to share,
Every stumble and mishap, a joy we declare.
A symphony of giggles, a playful embrace,
In this world of blunders, I've found my place.

## **Glistening Hope**

In the morning light, a coffee cup waits,
Steam spirals upward, just like my fates.
With caffeine in hand, I zoom like a jet,
Until the cat pounces, and I lose my bet.

The toast pops up with a joyful surprise,
A minor explosion, what a day to rise!
I chase down my breakfast, a curious dance,
While crumbs shimmy down in a fairy-like trance.

My dog shoots past like a furry cannonball,
Chasing his tail, he's having a ball.
He's plotting his takeover, I see the signs,
As I sip on my coffee, while crossing the lines.

Hope glimmers bright, lighting up the room,
Amidst every clatter, there's laughter's sweet bloom.
In this merry chaos, joy floats in the air,
With each silly moment, life's treasures we share.

## **Starry-Eyed Vigil**

Under the stars, I sit with my pie,
A perfect distraction, oh me, oh my.
The moon winks at me, in a mischievous way,
As fireflies flicker, like they're ready to play.

Suddenly I hear a soft rustling sound,
It's my dog on a mission, loose on the ground.
He leaps after shadows that dart here and there,
In a quest for adventure, without a care.

The neighbors look out, with concerned little frowns,
Wondering why this brave pup wears no crowns.
He's just on a spree, living life to the max,
While I munch on my pie, with crumbs on my slacks.

So here in the night, where laughter runs free,
I treasure these moments, just my pie and me.
For under the starlight, with mischief aglow,
Life's funniest tales always seem to grow.

www.ingramcontent.com/pod-product-compliance
Lightning Source LLC
Chambersburg PA
CBHW051732290426
43661CB00123B/247